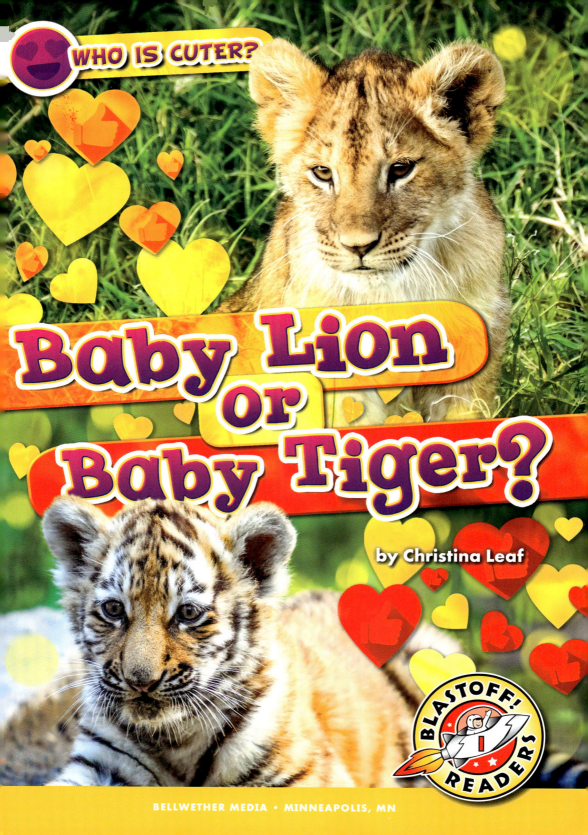

Blastoff! Readers are carefully developed by literacy experts to build reading stamina and move students toward fluency by combining standards-based content with developmentally appropriate text.

Level 1 provides the most support through repetition of high-frequency words, light text, predictable sentence patterns, and strong visual support.

Level 2 offers early readers a bit more challenge through varied sentences, increased text load, and text-supportive special features.

Level 3 advances early-fluent readers toward fluency through increased text load, less reliance on photos, advancing concepts, longer sentences, and more complex special features.

★ **Blastoff! Universe**

This edition first published in 2025 by Bellwether Media, Inc.

No part of this publication may be reproduced in whole or in part without written permission of the publisher. For information regarding permission, write to Bellwether Media, Inc., Attention: Permissions Department, 6012 Blue Circle Drive, Minnetonka, MN 55343.

Library of Congress Cataloging-in-Publication Data

Names: Leaf, Christina, author.
Title: Baby lion or baby tiger? / by Christina Leaf.
Description: Minneapolis, MN : Bellwether Media, Inc., 2025. | Series: Blastoff! readers: who is cuter? | Includes bibliographical references and index. | Audience: Ages 5-8 | Audience: Grades K-1 | Summary: "Developed by literacy experts for students in kindergarten through grade three, this book introduces the differences between baby lions and baby tigers to young readers through leveled text and related photos"– Provided by publisher.
Identifiers: LCCN 2024003097 (print) | LCCN 2024003098 (ebook) | ISBN 9798886870329 (library binding) | ISBN 9798893041460 (paperback) | ISBN 9781644878767 (ebook)
Subjects: LCSH: Lion–Juvenile literature. | Tiger–Juvenile literature. | Lion–Infancy–Juvenile literature. | Tiger–Infancy–Juvenile literature.
Classification: LCC QL737.C23 L4198 2025 (print) | LCC QL737.C23 (ebook) | DDC 599.75/51392–dc23/eng/20240301
LC record available at https://lccn.loc.gov/2024003097
LC ebook record available at https://lccn.loc.gov/2024003098

Text copyright © 2025 by Bellwether Media, Inc. BLASTOFF! READERS and associated logos are trademarks and/or registered trademarks of Bellwether Media, Inc. Bellwether Media is a division of Chrysalis Education Group.

Editor: Suzane Nguyen   Designer: Andrea Schneider

Printed in the United States of America, North Mankato, MN.

Table of Contents

Lion Cubs and Tiger Cubs!	4
Spots and Stripes	8
Home Life	14
Who Is Cuter?	20
Glossary	22
To Learn More	23
Index	24

Lion Cubs and Tiger Cubs!

Baby lions and baby tigers have the same name. They are both cubs!

lion cubs

tiger cubs

These babies are both in the cat family.

Spots and Stripes

Lion cubs are tan.
Tiger cubs are orange!

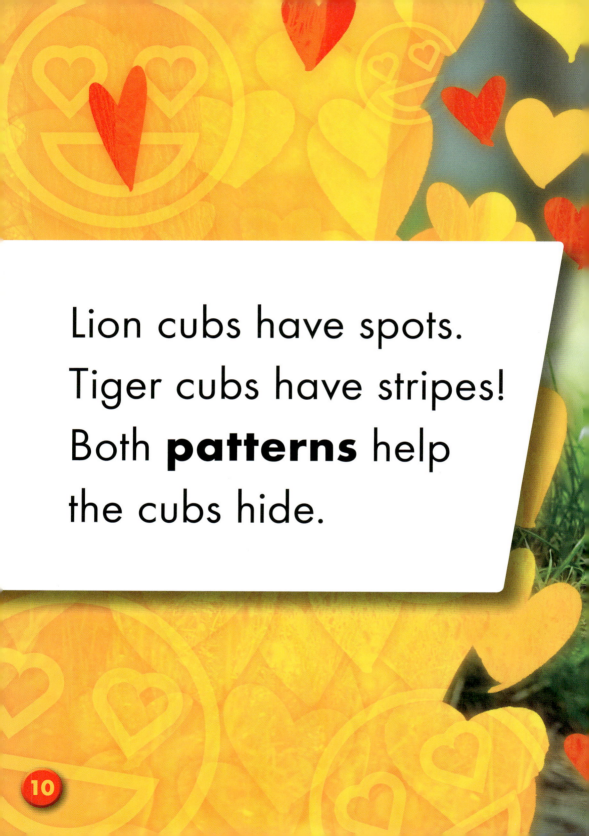

Lion cubs have spots. Tiger cubs have stripes! Both **patterns** help the cubs hide.

Lion cub tails have a black tip. Tiger cub tails are striped.

black tip

Home Life

Lion cubs mostly live in **savannas**. Tiger cubs call forests, savannas, and **swamps** home.

savanna

swamp

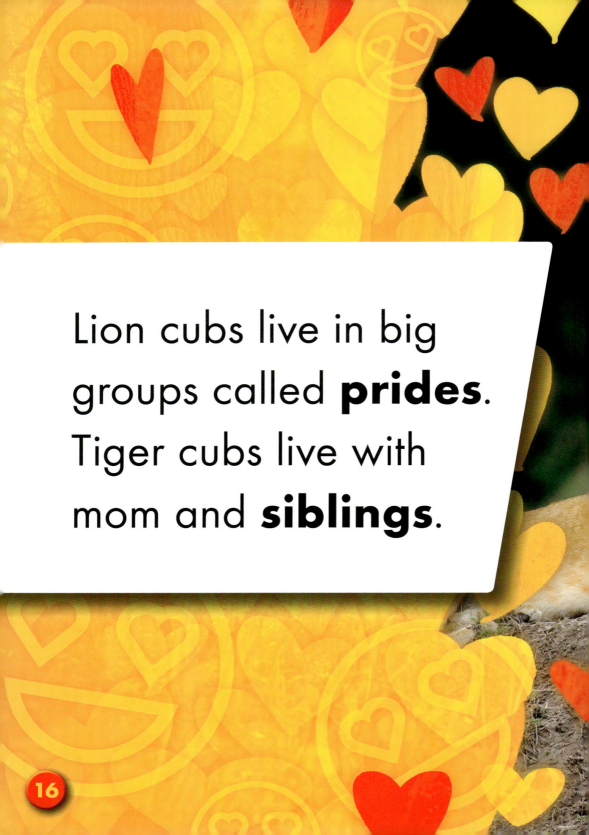

Lion cubs live in big groups called **prides**. Tiger cubs live with mom and **siblings**.

siblings

pride

Lion cubs do not like to swim. Tiger cubs do! Which one is cuter?

Who Is Cuter?

has spots

tan

black tip on tail

Baby Lion

mostly lives in savannas

lives in a pride

does not like to swim

Glossary

patterns
markings on an animal's fur

siblings
brothers and sisters

prides
groups of lions

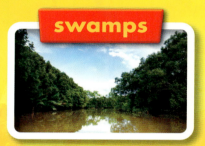

swamps
wetlands filled with trees and other woody plants

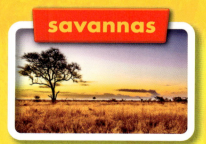

savannas
flat grasslands with few trees

To Learn More

AT THE LIBRARY

Cutest Animals on the Planet. Washington, D.C.: National Geographic, 2021.

Neuenfeldt, Elizabeth. *Baby Lions*. Minneapolis, Minn.: Bellwether Media, 2024.

Rathburn, Betsy. *Baby Tigers*. Minneapolis, Minn.: Bellwether Media, 2024.

ON THE WEB

FACTSURFER

Factsurfer.com gives you a safe, fun way to find more information.

1. Go to www.factsurfer.com.

2. Enter "baby lion or baby tiger" into the search box and click 🔍.

3. Select your book cover to see a list of related content.

Index

cat family, 6
colors, 8, 12, 13
forests, 14
hide, 10
lions, 4
mom, 16
name, 4
patterns, 10
prides, 16, 17
savannas, 14, 15
siblings, 16, 17
spots, 10, 11
stripes, 10, 11, 12
swamps, 14, 15
swim, 18
tails, 12
tigers, 4

The images in this book are reproduced through the courtesy of: Chris Taylor, front cover (lion); Zhiltsov Alexandr, front cover (tiger); Eric Isselee, pp. 3 (lion), 20 (lion), 21 (tiger); Anan Kaewkhammul, p. 3 (tiger); Theodore Mattas, pp. 4-5; Sarah Cheriton-Jones/ Adobe Stock, p. 5; Daria Dmitrieva, pp. 6-7; John Loss, p. 7; Rudi Hulshof, pp. 8-9; Richard C10, p. 9; Eric Gevaert/ Adobe Stock, pp. 10-11; Stu Porter, p. 11; Henk Bogaard/ Getty Images, pp. 12-13; Alexander Zhiltsov/ Adobe Stock pp. 13; Frank11, pp. 14-15; kyslynskahal, p. 15; GUDKOV ANDREY, pp. 16-17; dpa picture alliance / Alamy Stock Photo/ Alamy, p. 17; Avalon.red / Alamy Stock Photo/ Alamy, pp. 18-19; Mauritz Janeke / 500px/ Getty Images, p. 19; Simon Dannhauer, p. 20 (mostly lives in savannas); Ashley Solle, p. 20 (lives in a pride); Reto Buehler, p. 20 (does not like to swim); Aleksandr Lavrinenko, p. 21 (lives in forests, savannas, and swamps); Sourabh Bharti, p. 21 (lives with mom and siblings); James Warwick/ Getty Images, p. 21 (likes to swim); dangdumrong, p. 22 (patterns); John Michael Vosloo, p. 22 (prides); Harry Beugelink, p. 22 (savannas); Dr Ajay Kumar Singh, p. 22 (siblings); Sylvia sooyoN, p. 22 (swamps).